On the Wing 翅膀

North American Birds 5

Andrea Voon

Richard Han

大翅膀，大翅膀扇呀扇，
Dà chì bǎng dà chì bǎng shàn ya shàn

沼澤裏的 環保人員 真浪漫。
zhǎo zé li de huán bǎo rén yuán zhēn làng màn

綠翅鴨，綠翅鴨 喜結良緣，
Lù chì yā lù chì yā xǐ jié liáng yuán

拍動翅膀一飛衝天。
pāi dòng chì bǎng yì fēi chōng tiān

Great big wings, great big wings, flap flap flap...
Recycling agents in the marshes are on the wing.

Green-winged Teals, Green-winged Teals, clap clap clap...
Lift their wings and take-off straight in the spring.

2

Dà chì bǎng　　dà chì bǎng shàn ya shàn

大翅膀，大翅膀扇呀扇，

zhǎo zé li de　　kōng fú yuán　zhēn làng màn

沼澤裏的 空服員 真浪漫。

Lán chì yā　　　guì hóng yā　　xǐ jié liáng yuán

藍翅鴨，桂紅鴨 喜結良緣，

qǐ chéng qiān yí lù tú yáo yuǎn

啓程遷移路途遥远。

Great big wings, great big wings, flap flap flap…

Flight attendants in the marshes are on the wing.

Blue-winged Teals, Cinnamon Teals, clap clap clap…

Take-off early for migration in the spring.

Dà chì bǎng   dà chì bǎng shàn ya shàn
大翅膀，大翅膀扇呀扇，

hú pō li de   tiào shuǐ xuǎn shǒu   zhēn làng màn
湖泊裹的　跳水選手　真浪漫。

Huán jǐng qián yā   huán jǐng qián yā   xǐ jié liáng yuán
環頸潛鴨，環頸潛鴨 喜結良緣，

lì   sè jǐng wén ruò yǐn ruò xiàn
栗色頸紋若隱若現。

Great big wings, great big wings, flap flap flap…

Divers in the lakes and ponds are on the wing.

Ring-necked Ducks, Ring-necked Ducks, clap clap clap…

Leap and plunge underwater in the spring.

6

大翅膀，大翅膀扇呀扇，

湖泊裏的 武林高手 真浪漫。

美洲白冠雞，美洲白冠雞 喜結良緣，

水上奔跑，輕功不凡。

Great big wings, great big wings, flap flap flap…

Kung fu masters in the lakes and ponds are on the wing.

American Coots, American Coots, clap clap clap…

Run on water and muddy ground in the spring.

大翅膀，大翅膀扇呀扇，

湖泊裏的 俳舞舞蹈員 真浪漫。

鬃林鴨，鬃林鴨 喜結良緣，

爬樹築巢栖于樹幹。

Great big wings, great big wings, flap flap flap...

Powwow dancers in the lakes and ponds are on the wing.

Wood Ducks, Wood Ducks, clap clap clap...

Perch and climb on tree branches in the spring.

Dà chì bǎng　　dà chì bǎng shàn ya shàn

大翅膀，大翅膀扇呀扇，

lái zì dōng yà de　　xì qǔ yǎn yuán　zhēn làng màn

來自東亞的　戲曲演員　真浪漫。

Yuān yāng　　yuān yāng　xǐ jié liáng yuán

鴛鴦，鴛鴦 喜結良緣，

yǔ guàn　fān　yǔ guāng xiān míng yàn

羽冠、帆羽光鮮明艷。

Great big wings, great big wings, flap　flap flap…

Chinese opera actors from East Asia are on the wing.

Mandarin Ducks, Mandarin Ducks, clap clap clap…

Raise their crest and show of "sail" feathers in the spring.

大翅膀，大翅膀扇呀扇，

湖泊裏的 蛤蜊採收員 真浪漫。

小斑背潛鴨，斑背潛鴨 喜結良緣，

挖蛤的扁嘴呈灰藍。

Great big wings, great big wings, flap flap flap...

Clam diggers in the lakes and ponds are on the wing.

Lesser Scaups, Greater Scaups, clap clap clap...

Forage on the soft mud in the spring.

Dà chì bǎng   dà chì bǎng shàn ya shàn
大翅膀，大翅膀扇呀扇，

hú pō li de   pèi jìng shī   zhēn làng màn
湖泊裏的 配鏡師 真浪漫。

Què yā   què yā   xǐ jié liáng yuán
鵲鴨，鵲鴨 喜結良緣，

qiú ǒu dòng zuò fù zá duō biàn
求偶動作複雜多變。

Great big wings, great big wings, flap flap flap…
Opticians in the lakes and ponds are on the wing.
Common Goldeneyes, Common Goldeneyes, clap clap clap…
Perform a set of courtship moves in the spring.

大翅膀，大翅膀扇呀扇，

沼澤裏的 導游 真浪漫。

赤膀鴨，赤膀鴨 喜結良緣，

搶奪食物欺負同伴。

Great big wings, great big wings, flap flap flap…

Tour guides in the marshes are on the wing.

Gadwalls, Gadwalls, clap clap clap…

Steal food from diving ducks in the spring.

大翅膀，大翅膀扇呀扇，

湖泊裏的 園藝師 真浪漫。

綠眉鴨，赤頸鴨 喜結良緣，

採摘植物頭禿喙短。

Great big wings, great big wings, flap flap flap…

Landscapers in the lakes and ponds are on the wing.

American Wigeons, Eurasian Wigeons, clap clap clap…

Pluck and nibble plants in the spring.

Dà chì bǎng   dà chì bǎng shàn ya shàn
大翅膀，大翅膀扇呀扇，

zhǎo zé li de   jiào shī   zhēn làng màn
沼澤裏的 教師 真浪漫。

Zhēn wěi yā   zhēn wěi yā   xǐ jié liáng yuán
針尾鴨，針尾鴨 喜結良緣，

cháng cháng de   wěi yǔ zhēn qiǎng yǎn
長長的尾羽真搶眼。

Great big wings, great big wings, flap flap flap...

Teachers in the marshes are on the wing.

Northern Pintails, Northern Pintails, clap clap clap...

Dabble and swim with their pointy tail in the spring.

Dà chì bǎng   dà chì bǎng shàn ya shàn
大翅膀，大翅膀扇呀扇，

hú pō li de   zuò jiā   zhēn làng màn
湖泊裏的 作家 真浪漫。

Yóu bí tiān é   yóu bí tiān é   xǐ jié liáng yuán
疣鼻天鵝，疣鼻天鵝 喜結良緣，

wēi tí chì bǎng suí fēng yáng fān
微提翅膀隨風揚帆。

Great big wings, great big wings, flap flap flap...

Authors in the lakes and ponds are on the wing.

Mute Swans, Mute Swans, clap clap clap...

Raise their wing and sail elegantly in the spring.

Shuǐ qín　　shuǐ qín　　shàn ya shàn

水禽，水禽 扇呀扇，

qiān lǐ yīn yuán yí xiàn qiān

千里姻緣一綫牽。

Yí jì qíng rén　　zhōng shēn bàn lǚ　　xǐ jié liáng yuán

一季情人，終身伴侶 喜結良緣，

bǐ yì shuāng fēi　　qíng yì mián mián

比翼雙飛，情意綿綿。

Waterfowl, waterfowl, flap flap flap…

Find their perfect match on the wing.

Seasonal partners, lifelong partners, clap clap clap…

Prepare for the breeding season in the spring.

作者 Author

温甘玉芬

當媽前，她是孩子們的甘老師，在常年暖和的熱帶雨林，與孩子一起學習中、英文，探索文字的奧秘；當媽後，她是孩子們的溫媽咪，在四季分明的北半球，與孩子一起感受春夏秋冬的更替，一起尋找美好的童年……

溫媽咪創作的靈感，源自於多年來的童言童語。
2021年，她成立了"溫室工作坊"，立志要出版一系列的中、英雙語繪本，結合母語和第二語言，提倡親子趣讀。精通三語的溫媽咪理解每一種語言都有其獨特的藝術形式，因此創作的雙語繪本也各含韻味、各具特色。

Andrea Voon

Over the past few years, Andrea has learned and grown with her family as a full-time mother in Canada. Back in Malaysia, she was a Chinese immersion elementary school teacher. In 2021, Andrea started her journey as an author. Growing up in a multilingual environment, Andrea loves the beauty of languages on their own. She has the vision to publish picture books to support bilingual families in raising their children in English, Cantonese, and Chinese reading.

攝影師 Photographer

Richard Han

Richard loves to practice patience through his lenses of the natural world. He enjoys observing the wildlife and photographing the natural lifestyles that animals live. He is excited to present the beautiful photos that he captured in dreamy tones and colors to all the birds lover.

溫室工作坊

BILINGUAL READING IS FUN!

Check out other bilingual picture books by Andrea Voon.

To **Shirley Han, Derek, Eliana, Alayna & Magnus Dominus**

with love -- Andrea. V

For **Richard Han**

The patience in natural photography

ISBN 978-1-998856-43-5

Text copyright © 2024 Andrea Voon

Picture Credit © 2024 Richard Han